Marti
King Jr.

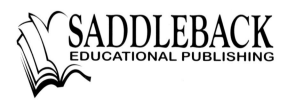
SADDLEBACK
EDUCATIONAL PUBLISHING

Saddleback's Graphic Biographies

SADDLEBACK
EDUCATIONAL PUBLISHING
www.sdlback.com

ISBN-13: 978-1-59905-227-4
ISBN-10: 1-59905-227-X
eBook: 978-1-60291-590-9

Printed in Guangzhou, China
0610/06-52-10

13 12 11 10 3 4 5 6 7 8 9

Martin Luther King Jr. loved to listen to his father preach. His father told the people to hold their heads high and always walk with God.

Some day I'm going to have some big words too!

I have a dream that my four children will one day live in a nation where they will be judged by their character—not by the color of their skin.

Martin Luther King Jr. did learn big and powerful words. He spoke before two hundred thousand people in Washington, D.C. Millions saw and heard him on television.

Chapter I The Early Years

Martin Luther King Jr. was born January 15, 1929, in Atlanta, Georgia. His father was minister of the Ebenezer Baptist Church.

Most of the time, Martin or M.L. as he was called, played well with his brother and sister.

Their parents often told them that there was nothing more important than loving one another.

Why do you work?

To buy books. We have to earn our own spending money.

From the time he could lift papers, Martin delivered the *Atlanta Journal.*

Once your grandfather wanted a new high school for African Americans, and a newspaper wrote bad things about it, so he asked people not to buy the paper.

From his family, Martin learned about family history, the Bible, and things people could do if they worked together.

Martin was six when learned about prejudice. His mother comforted him.

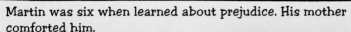

Always remember you are as good as anyone.

His white friend's mother had told Martin that he was no longer welcome because he was an African American.

Martin's mother told him about slavery and how hard life had always been for black people in this country.

Martin's father had worked in the fields with his family.

At sixteen he went to Atlanta to work in a railroad yard. For years he worked during the day and went to school at night. He finally became a minister.

Let's see your license, boy.

I am a man. This is a boy.

You must sit in the back.

If you cannot wait on us here, we do not want to buy.

Martin's father was not afraid to speak up.

Martin went to a public speaking contest. Because the bus was crowded he was ordered to give up his seat. At first Martin didn't budge.

Move back or I'll call the police.

Martin had to stand for almost two hours. He felt it was unfair.

At fifteen, he entered Morehouse College.

At seventeen, Martin preached his first sermon. At eighteen he was made assistant pastor. At nineteen he graduated from college.

In 1948 Martin went to Crozer Theological Seminary in Chester, Pennsylvania. There were only six African Americans in a class of one hundred.

This is hard to believe— eating in a white restaurant!

Not all places in the North admit African Americans.

In 1951 Martin Luther King Jr. received his master's degree from Crozer and a scholarship to Boston University. He met Coretta Scott in Boston.

Coretta Scott's father had worked and built a fine sawmill.

I'm sorry but the mill is not for sale.

Well, it won't do you any good!

The next Sunday, while the Scotts were at church, the sawmill burned down.

Like Martin, Coretta also had learned early what it meant to be black.

Why do we have to walk?

Never mind. Let's sing while we walk.

Later, Coretta went on to Antioch College in Ohio.

She sang well and won a scholarship to the New England Conservatory of Music.

If you keep the fifth floor clean, I will give you your room and breakfast.

I want a career in music.

I want a beautiful wife with a beautiful voice. You!

Quiet Coretta fell in love with outgoing Martin. She knew his wishes would always come first.

But now ... three people had different dreams of the future.

Martin and I will live in the North, so I can sing.

Coretta and I will live in the South. I will have my own church.

Martin will preach in Atlanta with me.

On June 18, 1953, Martin Luther King Jr. married Coretta Scott in Alabama.

Will they return to Boston?

Yes. Coretta will continue her voice training, and Martin will work for his doctorate.

When he was twenty-five, Martin became pastor of the Dexter Avenue Church in Montgomery, Alabama.

I'm proud that you have your own church.

I'll be proud when you sing solos here.

In Montgomery, Martin met the Reverend Ralph Abernathy.

We are so different. You love to study.

You are full of fun. I need your friendship.

Chapter II The Bus Boycott

To segregate means to separate, like keeping white sheep away from black sheep in a flock. When Dr. King went to Alabama, there were rules about segregating.

No blacks allowed here.

Black children can't go to parks for whites.

No blacks allowed through the front entrance.

Blacks had to use the back door and sit in the balcony.

This school is for whites only.

We only serve white people. Servants traveling with white customers are fed in the kitchen.

Some white people called black people "Jim Crows." The Jim Crow Laws covered drinking fountains, bathrooms, buses, etc. It was the way segregation and discrimination* was kept alive.

* prejudiced outlook, action, or treatment

8

In 1863 Abraham Lincoln declared that slaves were free. But in fact, African Americans were not always treated as citizens.

You can only register to vote if a white person signs for you. And they won't.

Southern whites made local laws to keep blacks from voting.

I have a college degree.

Won't do you much good.

It was hard for an African American to get a decent job.

They didn't listen to my side.

They always find the black person guilty.

Don't worry, the police won't bother us!

It's not fair for us to pay at the front and then have to hurry to the back to get on.

Yes, sometimes the driver takes your money and shuts the door on you.

African Americans could sit from the back up through the fifth row, if there weren't any whites who needed seats.

Give this white man your seat and go stand in the back.

On December 1, 1955, Rosa Parks, tired after a hard day's work, rode home on a Montgomery, Alabama, bus.

Because Rosa quietly refused to move, the driver called the police.

You are breaking a city law.

Rosa Parks was arrested. We will boycott* the bus on Monday. Black people will not ride the Montgomery buses.

Dr. King and others agreed to help by writing letters telling black people about the boycott. Students delivered them.

My maid can't read and gave me an upsetting letter to read to her. I want it published.

The newspaper published the letter and more people learned about the boycott.

Martin, come quickly! The bus is empty. The boycott is working.

* to act together in refusal to have dealings with (as a person, store, or organization)

At this rally, Dr. King first spoke about nonviolence.

We will not support a bad system. We will continue the boycott, but we must be peaceful. Jesus taught us to love our enemies.

But there was violence. The King's house was bombed. Dr. King calmed the angry crowd.

We are safe. Please go home peacefully.

Dr. King had work to do and stayed in Montgomery.

Daddy, you worry too much.

Your lives are in danger! Please come back to Atlanta.

Money came from all over the country to help. The boycott continued. Montgomery businessmen complained. Because of TV, newspaper, and magazine stories, MIA became famous. In May, there was a freedom rally at Madison Square Garden in New York City.

That's Eleanor Roosevelt.

There are Hollywood stars and all kinds of famous people!

The city of Montgomery tried to say that carpools used by blacks were not lawful. There was a court hearing in November 1956.

Because he was a boycott leader, Dr. King had to go to court. While there, he heard great news.

The United States Supreme Court declared segregation on public transportation to be illegal.

In Montgomery, blacks waited for the Supreme Court order to be sent officially to the city. In churches and schools, they practiced how to ride buses peacefully.

The people with arm bands are white.

Be polite. Always say, "May I?" or "Pardon me." as you sit.

Don't sit here!

No! No! Don't hit back! Move away from trouble.

On December 12, 1956, the boycott was over. It had lasted over a year.

Good morning, and welcome, Dr. King.

Chapter III Sit-Ins and Freedom Rides

Dr. and Mrs. King visited the Gold Coast of Africa when Ghana gained its independence from Great Britain.

Blacks now own and govern their own land!

And African Americans can lend their technical assistance to a growing new nation.

You know of the bus boycott in Montgomery?

You are known and respected the world over.

A group of ministers formed the Southern Christian Leadership Conference (SCLC).

But we must also remember blacks in the North and West.

The National Association for the Advancement of Colored People (NAACP) organized a prayer pilgrimage* to Washington. Over 30,000 people joined. Dr. King spoke last.

Give us the right to vote and we will write proper laws.

The crowd cheered Dr. King. They wanted him to keep talking. He was their leader, following in the footsteps of Jesus and Gandhi.

* any long journey to a shrine or sacred place

In 1959 the Kings visited India, the country of Mahatma Gandhi.

They met Prime Minister Nehru.

You know more about Gandhi than many Hindus.

He walked hundreds of miles to get salt from the sea. It was a peaceful protest against the salt tax.

Without using violence, he freed his people from British rule.

At thirty-one, Dr. King lived with praise and criticism. To devote full time to the SCLC, he left his church and returned to Atlanta in January 1960.

A black Gandhi.

With ten whites for every black, we cannot win with violence. Our weapon must be love.

A Communist.

He's trying to be white.

Just another radical.

He taught us to lift our heads up!

A great human being.

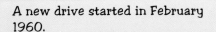

A new drive started in February 1960.

In North Carolina, we do not serve African Americans.

You want us to buy things from you but won't let us eat here?

Four days later, white students joined them.

We cannot serve black people.

Then we'll sit with them without ordering.

A reporter wrote of the sit-ins. Soon black and white college students all over the South were having sit-ins at local restaurants.

I admire your peaceful ways. The SCLC will help.

We call ourselves the Student Nonviolent Coordinating Committee, SNCC for short.

I've been good to blacks.

The SNCC students became role models for an entire generation of young activists from across the United States.

You let us buy here but your store is segregated. We can't eat here.

In May, "Freedom Rides" were organized. Whites and blacks boarded buses and rode through the South. They sat together at restaurants.

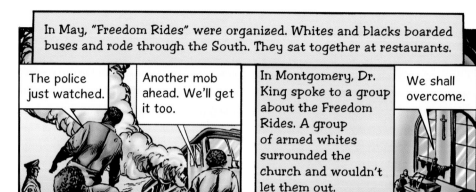

The police just watched.

Another mob ahead. We'll get it too.

In Montgomery, Dr. King spoke to a group about the Freedom Rides. A group of armed whites surrounded the church and wouldn't let them out.

We shall overcome.

In Alabama, whites attacked the passengers.

Attorney General Robert Kennedy ordered the governor of Alabama to protect them while exiting.

The Freedom Rides were successful. The United States government said that segregation was against the law on buses, trains, and in waiting rooms.

Dr. King urged black leaders to work together.

More action.

NAACP

NATIONAL ASSOCIATION ADVANCEMENT COLORED PEOPLE

Work through the courts for new laws.

SNCC STUDENT NON-VIOLENT COORDIN[...] COMMIT[...]

CORE CONGRESS OF RACIAL EQUALITY -1942-

URBAN LEAGUE FOUNDED IN 1910

Better education and better jobs for African Americans.

Better jobs!

Chapter IV The Birmingham Marches

In April 1963 Dr. King led a protest in Birmingham, Alabama. White people had been very harsh to blacks in this Southern city.

Reverend Abernathy and I will lead a march on Good Friday.

Your thirteenth arrest!

But when we're jailed together, you keep up my spirits.

They were arrested for demonstrating without a permit.

But this time, Dr. King was put in a cell by himself. He was not allowed visitors or phone calls. A group of Protestant, Catholic, and Jewish clergymen wrote a letter to a newspaper calling the demonstration march "unwise."

I must remind these men of God that they are unwise to forget the terrible conditions of blacks in Birmingham.

Dr. King's "Letter from a Birmingham Jail" has been reprinted many times.

Coretta Scott King was worried about what might happen to her husband in jail. She even tried to call the president. Then she received two important phone calls.

The president just called back to tell me the F.B.I. is checking on Martin.

Singer Harry Belafonte was also worried about Martin. He raised money to help.

Martin gives most of his money to the movement.

After Dr. King's release, Attorney General Robert Kennedy made two phone calls.

I wish you'd ease up on your protests, Dr. King.

But sir, the black man has already waited three hundred years.

Governor Wallace, the courts will demand that you allow African Americans in white schools.

Never! I am completely in favor of segregation.

In jail, Dr. King had decided to let children join the protest for better conditions in Birmingham.

The first volunteers were sent to a white library.

They have some nerve!

FOR WHITES ONLY

I'm proud of you. When they locked the gates at your school, you climbed the fence to get here.

About one thousand children gathered in the church. Police were posted outside. The children left in small groups and agreed to meet downtown.

The police can't round them up.

But as the children gathered to march downtown, police made arrests.

How old are you?

Seven.

The next day, the cruel orders of Police Commissioner "Bull" Connor were carried out.

As the children left the church, they were knocked down by water from firemen's hoses. Attack dogs were even used against them.

Take your weapons and go home! Your children don't need more violence!

Bull Connor hated blacks and didn't care who knew it.

A riot was prevented.

Look at what they are doing to the children.

God help us! Is this the United States?

All over America, people were shocked by what they saw.

Blacks tried to attend services in twenty-one white churches.

We, too, are Christians.

Only white people can worship here.

Only four churches admitted blacks.

When fire hoses were pointed at his group, Reverend Billups told them to kneel and pray.

Turn on those hoses!

But the firemen refused to use hoses, and police refused to let the dogs loose.

President Kennedy's cabinet members urged Birmingham businessmen to make peace.

We have come to an agreement with the city. No more segregation. There will be more and better jobs for blacks.

On June 11, 1963, President John F. Kennedy went before the TV cameras. He talked to the American people about civil rights.

This nation will not be fully free until all citizens have equal rights.

Chapter V I Have A Dream

Inspired by Birmingham, peaceful marches were held in over 800 cities.

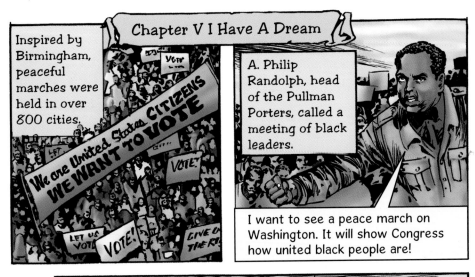

A. Philip Randolph, head of the Pullman Porters, called a meeting of black leaders.

I want to see a peace march on Washington. It will show Congress how united black people are!

The march on Washington was August 28, 1963. 250,000 people from all over the United States joined in. There were many white people there too!

It was a great and happy event. And the last speech given by the Reverend Martin Luther King Jr. will never be forgotten.

I have a dream that one day on the red hills of Georgia, the sons of former slaves and the sons of former slave owners will be able to sit down together at the table of brotherhood.

Some progress was made. Some restaurants became desegregated. Some African American found better jobs. But there was more bloodshed.

In September, a black church in Birmingham was bombed. Four black children were killed.

On November 22, 1963, President Kennedy was assassinated.

That's how I will go too.

In January 1964 Dr. King was named Man of the Year by *Time* magazine.

This is a tribute to the freedom movement.

In July 1964 President Lyndon Johnson, a Southerner, forced the Civil Rights Bill through the U.S. Congress.

The pen goes to Dr. King.

In October 1964 the Norwegian Nobel Committee announced that Dr. King won the Nobel Peace Prize.

He and his family flew to Norway. At thirty-five, he was the youngest person ever to receive the award.

Now the King family will go down in world history as well as American history.

In Selma, Alabama, Sheriff Jim Clark wanted blacks to stay in "Colored Town."

We wish to register to vote.

Go back where you belong.

In March 1965 Dr. King led a five-day march from Selma to Montgomery to ask for the right to vote.

There are 20,000 of us.

Many famous people, too—white and black.

President Johnson urged Congress to pass a voting rights bill.

We must overcome injustice to African Americans. All of our citizens need to vote.

Dr. King made a speech and hoped Governor Wallace heard it.

If the white man uses clubs against us, we will make him do it in the glaring light of television.

The Voting Rights Act was signed by President Johnson in the summer of 1965.

Today is a triumph for freedom.

Every black adult now has the right to vote. No state can use tricks to stop us.

In 1966 Dr. King went to Chicago. He found living conditions for blacks to be very bad.

And our rent is high!

Rats attack our babies.

Mayor Daly was a smart politician.

I don't want riots here! I'll pass an open housing bill letting blacks live wherever they want.

Although Dr. King was devoting all his time to civil rights, many blacks were impatient.

During long hot summers riots and looting took place.

Dr. King spoke against the Vietnam War. This made President Johnson angry.

Many leaders feel civil rights and peace movements do not mix.

I am against our being in Vietnam. I have to speak out.

Congress is not improving living conditions for blacks.

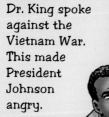

We'll lead a Poor People's Campaign on Washington and ask help for all of the poor including American Indians, Puerto Ricans, Mexicans, and even poor whites.

While Dr. King was planning the Poor People's Campaign, he was asked to go to Memphis, Tennessee.

At thirty-nine, Dr. King was tired. He traveled 10,000 miles a month to give speeches and lead marches. But he was always against violence.

One day in Memphis, it rained too hard for garbage men to work. Only the white workers were allowed to remain on the job and be paid.

The city isn't fair to black workers!

I agree! I will join your protest!

On April 4, 1968, Dr. King was shot and killed by James Earl Ray.

Coretta Scott King told the children that their father was dead but that his spirit would always remain alive.

The nation and the world mourned his death. 200,000 people marched in tribute and sang the freedom song, "We Shall Overcome."

On his final resting place were the words of an old slave song, "Free at last, Free at last, Thank God Almighty, I'm free at last."

Steadily and firmly, Martin Luther King Jr. led the way to freedom, opening the eyes and hearts of Americans. He had shared his dream with the world.

The END

Saddleback's Graphic Fiction & Nonfiction

If you enjoyed this Graphic Biography ... you will also enjoy our other graphic titles including:

Graphic Classics

- Around the World in Eighty Days
- The Best of Poe
- Black Beauty
- The Call of the Wild
- A Christmas Carol
- A Connecticut Yankee in King Arthur's Court
- Dr. Jekyll and Mr. Hyde
- Dracula
- Frankenstein
- The Great Adventures of Sherlock Holmes
- Gulliver's Travels
- Huckleberry Finn
- The Hunchback of Notre Dame
- The Invisible Man
- Jane Eyre
- Journey to the Center of the Earth
- Kidnapped
- The Last of the Mohicans
- The Man in the Iron Mask
- Moby Dick
- The Mutiny On Board H.M.S. Bounty
- The Mysterious Island
- The Prince and the Pauper
- The Red Badge of Courage
- The Scarlet Letter
- The Swiss Family Robinson
- A Tale of Two Cities
- The Three Musketeers
- The Time Machine
- Tom Sawyer
- Treasure Island
- 20,000 Leagues Under the Sea
- The War of the Worlds

Graphic Shakespeare

- As You Like It
- Hamlet
- Julius Caesar
- King Lear
- Macbeth
- The Merchant of Venice
- A Midsummer Night's Dream
- Othello
- Romeo and Juliet
- The Taming of the Shrew
- The Tempest
- Twelfth Night